ALL ABOUT
BUFFALO

By Maria Scrivani

Illustrations and design by Michael Morgulis

D1308573

Dedication

This book was inspired by a class of preschoolers at Kane Street Kids in Cobble Hill, Brooklyn, taught by my son, Devin Lipsitz. When I visited the students one sunny spring day, they had many questions about Buffalo – all weather-related. I told them there was much more to my hometown.

Here, then, is a book for children and the adults who love them – all about Buffalo.
          -Maria Scrivani

For my children and grandchildren, who have brought much color, light and joy to my life.
          -Michael Morgulis

This book was published and printed in Buffalo, N.Y. by Western New York Wares Inc.
Address all inquiries to:Western New York Wares, P.O. Box 733, Ellicott Station, Buffalo, N.Y. 14205

ISBN: 978-1-879201-70-5

Visit our Web site at www.buffalobooks.com

This is Buffalo,
a city on the western edge of New York State.

Looking at the 2010 United States Census,
you can see that Buffalo is the second most
populous city in the state.

ROCHESTER

UTICA

SYRACUSE

BUFFALO

ALBANY

NEW YORK CITY

Across the Peace Bridge
lies Canada, our friendly foreign neighbor.

From a spot in the Olmsted-designed Front Park
at the foot of Porter Avenue, you can see Canada
across the Peace Bridge.

**Native Americans
were the first people to make their homes here.**

Red Jacket, a Seneca leader and a famous orator,

is buried in Buffalo's Forest Lawn Cemetery,

where you can see his memorial today.

**Beside great Lake Erie
a village grew into a bustling port city.**

You can see the site of the old Erie Canal today
in the Canal Side development near the foot
of Main Street in downtown Buffalo.

In factories
steel was made, and grain milled into flour.

Drive along the waterfront in Buffalo's Old First
Ward and you can still see many examples
of the city's famous and much-photographed
grain elevators.

Buffalo today
is home to workers in hospitals and schools.

You can see the state-of-the-art Hauptman-
Woodward Medical Research Institute on Ellicott
Street in downtown Buffalo, one of several research
and health-related facilities that make up
the Buffalo Niagara Medical Campus.

Many cultures
mingle on streets, in parks and playgrounds.

You can see what African-American life was like in
early twentieth-century Buffalo in the Nash House.
This house museum is in downtown Buffalo near
the historic Michigan Street Baptist Church.

Winter snow
blankets ski trails and skating rinks.

See skaters enjoying the best of Buffalo winters
as they glide across Rotary Rink at Fountain Plaza,
the free public ice-skating rink in downtown Buffalo.

Spring flowers
bloom in backyards big and small.

See spring flowers blooming year-round in the
Buffalo and Erie County Botanical Gardens,
where a three-domed conservatory is the
pride of South Park, another Olmsted design.

Summer sun
smiles on sailors and swimmers.

Look for a different festival every weekend,
a feature of Buffalo summers. The Allentown Art
Festival is in early June. The National Buffalo Wing
Festival around Labor Day closes out the season.

**Fall foliage
leaves crunchy color under feet.**

See Delaware Park, the central jewel
of the Buffalo Olmsted parks system,
as it blazes with color every autumn.

**Fans follow sports,
festivals, art, music, theater and
awesome architecture.**

At the end of summer in Buffalo, you can visit
the Elmwood Festival of the Arts, held in the
vibrant Elmwood Village neighborhood.

All of this is Buffalo.

Look for the stone animals guarding the
perimeter of the Buffalo Zoo. Can you tell
what animal is sporting a snow mantle here?

MORE ABOUT BUFFALO

When you hear the name Buffalo, do you think of an animal?

The great shaggy beasts once ran in huge herds across the Western part of the United States, but probably never in Western New York. Still, the image of the animal remains the most popular symbol of our city. Just how did Buffalo get its name?

Some say it was named for a Native American, a fisherman who lived here for many years. Because of his long hair and large body, he was called by a name that in English means "buffalo." And so the place was called "Buffalo's Creek."

Another story is that Buffalo was named by French fur traders. When a hunting party went out to look for food, they could only find horses for meat. They came back to camp and said they had hunted down some "buffalo meat," a lie which may have led to the naming of a city.

Some believe there really had been a bison -- the other name for buffalo -- sighting in the area at one time. Perhaps it was a lone animal, separated from a herd which may have roamed as far as Pennsylvania (where buffalo bones have been found). The animal might have wandered to the salt-licks near Buffalo Creek.

Or perhaps someone simply mistook another big hairy animal here for a buffalo.

However it happened, a village was named.

Near the end of the eighteenth century, Native Americans from the Seneca Tribe lived along the shores of Lake Erie. French fur trappers, traveling near the mouth of Buffalo Creek, traded with the Senecas.

The land was a big forest, with very few people living nearby. By 1801, Holland Land Company surveyor Joseph Ellicott had set out a street plan for a town that was officially called New Amsterdam. At that time the land was owned by the Dutch.

In 1811, this frontier was the gateway to America's west, and the village was home to nearly 500 people, who called it Buffalo. It was across the lake from Fort Erie, which was then owned by the British. When Great Britain went to war against the United States of America in 1812, Buffalo was right in the middle of the fight.

Each country had native allies, and each attacked the other. At the end of 1813, a British raid ended in the burning of much of Buffalo. On New Year's Day, 1814, the invaders returned to finish the job, leaving just a few buildings standing.

Soon enough, the settlement with its hardy citizens rose again from the ashes of war. By the spring of 1815, the New York State Legislature had incorporated the Village of Buffalo.

A decade later, the Erie Canal opened in Buffalo, changing a sleepy village into a city of commerce. The canal linked the Great Lakes with the Atlantic Ocean.

By 1832, busy Buffalo had grown into a city.

Buffalo became a center for grain transport and storage. Midwestern grain was unloaded from lake boats onto canal boats headed to New York.

The work was made easier by the grain elevator, a steam-powered machine made by a Buffalo merchant. The machine lifted grain from ships into giant storage bins, some of which you can still see along the city's waterfront.

Workers in Buffalo at this time also had jobs in slaughterhouses, tanning and leather-making factories, banks and railroads, and flour and cereal mills. General Mills still manufactures Cheerios, Wheaties and Gold Medal Flour here.

The age of steel arrived in 1900. Buffalo was home to factories that made all kinds of metal products, and even automobiles. The Motorette, an auto made by Buffalo's Pierce Arrow Motor Car Company, was sold here at the Pan-American Exposition in 1901. Hydroelectric power from nearby Niagara Falls was first shown to the world at this great fair.

The expo was forever tarnished by the assassination of President William McKinley as he visited the Temple of Music. His successor took the presidential oath of office in Buffalo, at the Wilcox Mansion, now the Theodore Roosevelt Inaugural Site.

Though the fair ended tragically, Buffalo was still a great American city through the first half of the twentieth century.

In 1958, the St Lawrence Seaway was completed, and Buffalo was no longer the gateway for Great Lakes shipping to the Atlantic Ocean. Eventually, the great steel plants shut down.

The health care aides, teachers, research scientists, doctors, bankers, engineers, janitors, and a host of other kinds of workers who are Buffalonians today represent many different cultures. From its early days, Buffalo has attracted immigrants.

From westward-bound New Englanders to the Irish, who traveled from Canada to work along the Erie Canal, many ethnic groups came, running from war, looking for work and the chance for a new life.

Jews from Poland and Germany built synagogues, and African-Americans and Catholics from Italy and Poland built beautiful churches, still standing in old city neighborhoods.

By the middle of the twentieth century, Hungarians, Ukrainians, Greeks and Puerto Ricans were well-represented in Buffalo. Today's immigrants include Asian people like Vietnamese and Laotians, and lately, refugees from Africa such as Somalians. Local restaurants offer their food. Their holidays, language, clothing and customs enrich markets, street fairs and festivals. Their children learn English in our classrooms. Stitching strong new threads into the fabric of our community, they have all become Buffalonians.

Buffalo is beautiful in all seasons. The famous landscape architect Frederick Law Olmsted designed the citywide parks-and-parkway system. Delaware Park is the largest, and it's home to the Buffalo Zoo. This is where you can see a family of buffaloes.

Buffalo is well-known for its winters, thanks to an international headline-making blizzard in the winter of 1977. The truth is that Buffalo in recent years has not even earned the title of snowiest city in New York State, let alone the country. We do enjoy the snow when it comes, however.

Buffalo is also a great gardening town, as spring blooms throughout the various neighborhoods. In summer, the annual Garden Walk is a nationally-renowned event, as are the festivals that celebrate the arts and multiculturalism, practically every weekend. Beaches stretch from South Buffalo to the Canadian shore, and sailors and swimmers have ample opportunity to enjoy the area's pleasant summers.

In fall Buffalo's trees show their brightest colors in parks and along streets all around town.

Sports fans can follow Buffalo Bills football, Buffalo Sabres hockey, Buffalo Bisons baseball and Buffalo Bandits lacrosse.

Buffalo is home to the Albright-Knox Art Gallery, the Burchfield Penney Art Center, the Buffalo Museum of Science, and the Buffalo and Erie County Historical Society, as well as smaller museums and galleries. The Grammy Award-winning Buffalo Philharmonic Orchestra performs in one of the finest concert halls in the U.S., Kleinhans Music Hall.

Many stages feature live performances, from classic and new plays to touring Broadway musicals at Shea's Performing Arts Center.

All about Buffalo is also all about architecture. Few American cities have buildings that can compare with its landmarks. Fine examples of the work of our greatest architects have been preserved, from H.H. Richardson to Louis Sullivan, Stanford White and Frank Lloyd Wright.

About the publisher

Western New York's largest regional publishing company celebrated its 27th anniversary in 2011. It has distributed more than 300,000 books and other regional products into homes, schools and libraries since its inception.

The year was 1984 and the trivia craze was taking the nation by storm. As Buffalo journalist Brian Meyer played a popular trivia game with friends, he envisioned a game that tests players' knowledge about people and events in their hometown. Western New York Trivia Quotient sold out its first edition in six weeks and established Meyer as an up-and-coming young entrepreneur. A year later, he compiled a book of quotations that chronicled the feisty reign of the late Mayor Jimmy Griffin. Meyer has collaborated with dozens of authors, artists and photographers. By 2011, the company had been involved in publishing, marketing or distributing more than 180 regional products.

The Buffalo native is a graduate of the Marquette University, St. Joseph's Collegiate Institute and Buffalo Public School #56. He teaches communications courses at Buffalo State College and Medaille College. Meyer is treasurer of the Greater Buffalo Society of Professional Journalists' Scholarship Fund. Since 1991, Meyer has been assisted by Michele Ratzel, the company's business manager. The duo has nearly a half-century of combined experience in the regional publishing arena.

Other Books About Buffalo

Visit our Web site at <u>www.buffalobooks.com</u> for a complete list of titles distributed by Western New York Wares Inc.

Buffalo Snow

A full-color, beautifully illustrated children's book that tells the dramatic tale of a girl and her older brother stranded in a Buffalo whiteout. Created by Elizabeth Leader and Eve Tulbert, it's an inspiring story of how local residents open their homes and hearts to others.

ISBN: 978-1-4243-2471-2 **$6.95**

Brighter Buffalo: Renewing a City

This user-friendly guide to the Queen City's most iconic sites includes some new faces in town. Using archival photos, current images and a site map, author Maria Scrivani brings a fresh perspective to her hometown's architectural history.

ISBN: 978-1-879201-64-4 **$19.95**

Western New York 101: The 101 Greatest Moments in Buffalo History

From Father Baker's quest to build a shrine that would stand among the most beautiful in the country, to the Pan-American Exposition and the Erie Canal's opening, the region has been a home to history. Dan Murphy pinpoints 101 banner moments, supplementing his informative text with vintage photos.

ISBN: 978-1-879201-57-6 **$15.95**

Frank Lloyd Wright in Buffalo and Western New York

The region is home to one of the world's largest and most diverse collections of structures designed by America's most famous architect. Author Jan Sheridan takes a closer look at these prominent sites. Nearly 60 photographs and maps are included in this unique book.

ISBN: 1-978-1-879201-65-1 **$12.95**